URBAN LANDSCAPES

Industrial Landscape, Kearny, August, 1973

URBAN LANDSCAPES

A New Jersey Portrait

George A. Tice

RUTGERS UNIVERSITY PRESS, New Brunswick, New Jersey

BOOKS BY GEORGE A. TICE
FIELDS OF PEACE (*with Millen Brand*)
GOODBYE, RIVER, GOODBYE (*with George Mendoza*)
PATERSON
SEACOAST MAINE (*with Martin Dibner*)
GEORGE A. TICE / PHOTOGRAPHS / 1953-1973

Design: George A. Tice
Printing: Meriden Gravure Company
Paper: Warren's Lustro Offset Enamel Dull
Typography: Patrick & Highton
Type: Display, Bauer Bodoni; text, Bodoni
Binding: A. Horowitz & Son

Manufactured in the United States of America

Library of Congress Cataloging in Publication Data
Tice, George A
    Urban landscapes.

    1. New Jersey—Description and travel—1951-
—Views. I. Title.
F135.T52   917.49'04'40222   75-30549
ISBN 0-8135-0812-6
ISBN 0-8135-0813-4 pbk.

Triangle Sunoco Station, Route #46, South Hackensack, October, 1973

Woods, Madison Township, October, 1967

URBAN LANDSCAPES

Statement

Although people are not represented in this book by portraits, and appear only occasionally as small figures in a landscape, it is still a book about people's lives — about life in America in the 1970's. The setting is New Jersey. As I was born in New Jersey and still live there, I chose New Jersey's boundaries as my boundaries for working.

Having the entire state from which to select my pictures would, I believed, provide me with a larger choice of subjects than any one city or town could offer. It did, but attempting to cover the entire state was more a burden than a blessing. I might have done nearly everything I wanted to do, said everything I wanted to say, within a city such as Rahway, next to where I live. Actually I had considered a book on Rahway years earlier, but that project became PATERSON, which I may have stopped work on too soon. I regard URBAN LANDSCAPES as an extension of PATERSON.

Certain places I found so rich in material that they could have been the subjects of entire books. Besides Rahway, Atlantic City and Hoboken were especially attractive to me as a photographer. Some distressed cities I found too depressing to photograph. (I made five fruitless trips to Camden without ever setting up my camera.) As I progressed further with my project, it became obvious that it was really unimportant where I chose to photograph. The particular place simply provided an excuse to produce work.

My goal while photographing was to come up with at least one photograph from each day or evening I went exploring with my camera. Usually, I achieved that objective. When I didn't, I would question my creative ability and criticize myself for not being able to see. I have since learned that you can only see what you are ready to see — what mirrors your mind at that particular time.

This series has been a constant challenge. Frequently my problem was how to take interesting, expressive photographs of the most ordinary subjects, that I, for some intuitive reason, felt worthy of documentation. To accomplish this, I had to suppress my sense of familiarity with the subjects, so that I might perceive their own special qualities, and isolate them within the frame of my ground glass.

Looking at the photographs now, I am aware that I was not so detached as I had thought. Often I was looking back into my own past. Time, like light and presence, is locked in the images. I can recall sitting in an old coach diner on Sunday, drinking coffee and playing the juke box . . . having heels put on my shoes, while-u-wait . . . being fascinated with cemeteries, examining gravestones as one might art at a museum . . . thinking people who owned a Cadillac were rich . . . picking bouquets of pretty flowers from other people's gardens . . . wondering what people did in a Masonic Temple. Did they pray? . . . driving into gas stations at night for a dollar's worth of regular and asking for the key to the rest room . . . motels where I made love, registered as Mr. and Mrs. . . . knocking on doors of suburban houses trying to sell coupons for portrait sittings in natural color.

There is a certain measure of satisfaction in being able to document a place and express oneself simultaneously. The photographs are presented here as documents, but I am sure the art motive was primary, URBAN LANDSCAPES concerns my life as well as the lives of others. I hope all the pieces fit.

George A. Tice
January 17, 1975

To Shelley

Acknowledgments
I am indebted to the National Endowment for the Arts
and the John Simon Guggenheim Memorial Foundation
for their generous support of this project.

Railroad Bridge, High Bridge, April, 1974

Masonic Temple and Bell Drugs, Irving Street, Rahway, May, 1973

Living Room, Cleveland Avenue, Colonia, September, 1973

Holy Sepulchre Cemetery, Newark, April, 1974

Cosmopolitan Cleaners, French Street, New Brunswick, May, 1973

John's Bargain Store and Adam Hats, Broad Street, Elizabeth, July, 1972

Drawbridge, Morgan, September, 1973

Carteret Mobile Park, Carteret, November, 1973

Somerset County Courthouse, Main Street, Somerville, April, 1974

Hamilton Avenue, Paterson, April, 1971

Front Yard with Rose Bushes, Gadek Street, Perth Amboy, June, 1972

Monument Sweet Shop, Jersey Avenue, New Brunswick, May, 1973

The Central Jersey Bank and Trust Company, Freehold, February, 1974

Aspen Court, Paramus, October, 1973

Living Room with Christmas Tree, Rahway, December, 1973

Strand Theater, Front Street, Keyport, September, 1973

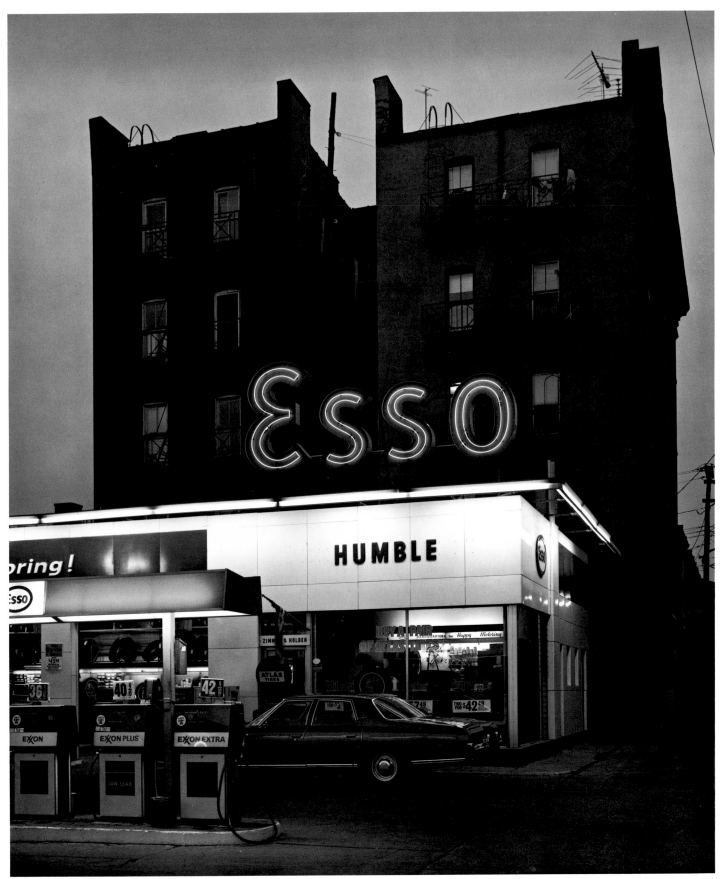

Esso Station and Apartment House, Willow Avenue, Hoboken, August, 1972

Dari D' Lite, Wood Avenue, Linden, October, 1973

Amusement Pier, Seaside Heights, June, 1972

Beach House, Lavallette, June, 1972

Bert's Shoe Repair, Wilson Avenue, Newark, May, 1973

The Manor Restaurant, Prospect Avenue, West Orange, August, 1973

Lexington Avenue, Passaic, October, 1973

Houses and Watertowers, East Main Street, Moorestown, December, 1973

Apartment House Lobby, South Munn Avenue, East Orange, July, 1973

Railroad Overpass, Van Houten Street, Paterson, September, 1970

Power Test Gas Station Rest Rooms, Route #1, Rahway, July, 1974

White Castle, Route #1, Rahway, September, 1973

Belmont Hotel, Asbury Avenue, Asbury Park, January, 1974

Interior, West Milton Avenue, Rahway, July, 1973

Twenty Two Byron Place, Colonia, April, 1974

St. George Diner, St. Georges Avenue, Linden, January, 1973

Smith's Used Furniture, Fayette Street, Perth Amboy, June, 1972

Downtown Newark: From Market Street, April, 1973

Dickinson High School, Jersey City, July, 1973

Goldy Pharmacy, Washington Street, Mount Holly, January, 1974

Jimmy's Bar & Grill and Conmar Zipper Company, Newark, May, 1973

Milton Meat Market, East Milton Avenue, Rahway, September, 1974

Oak Tree, Holmdel, May, 1970

Highway Sign, Route #34, Madison Township, February, 1974

Dill Avenue, Linden, February, 1974

Lackawanna Freight Station, Phillipsburg, June, 1973

Calvo's Beauty Shop and Boutique, Easton Avenue, New Brunswick, June, 1973

Garages, 16th Avenue, Irvington, December, 1974

Gar's Bakery and Leisure Laundry, Newark, December, 1974

The New International Cinema, Albany Street, New Brunswick, February, 1974

National Fuel Oil Company, Passaic Avenue, East Newark, March, 1973

Route #440 Overpass, Perth Amboy, December, 1973

Hudson's Fish Market and Absecon Lighthouse, Atlantic City, July, 1973

Petit's Mobil Station and Watertower, Cherry Hill, November, 1974

Castrol Motor Oil Company, Port Newark, July, 1973

Houses, Ocean Avenue, Ocean Grove, February, 1974

East Passaic Avenue, Nutley, April, 1973

Jahos Brothers Clothing Store, Broad Street, Trenton, April, 1973

Living Room, Chopin Drive, Hawthorne, April, 1973

Back Yard, Remsen Avenue, New Brunswick, November, 1973

The Pulaski Skyway, Jersey City, March, 1974

Atlantic Avenue, Atlantic City, September, 1973

Garden and 12th Streets, Hoboken, July, 1973

Cleveland Avenue, Colonia, April, 1973

House on Suydam Street, New Brunswick, February, 1974

House on Throckmorton Street, Freehold, February, 1974

12th Street, Hoboken, July, 1973

Back Yard Swimming Pool, Colonia Boulevard, Colonia, July, 1974

Lodi Circle Apartments, Route #46, Lodi, October, 1973

Living Room, Cooper Landing Road, Cherry Hill, December, 1974

Lake Terrace, Clark, April, 1974

Men's Room, Hotel Shelburne, Atlantic City, April, 1975

Steve's Diner, Route #130, North Brunswick, January, 1974

Main Street, Rahway, December, 1974

Public Service Electric and Gas Company, Harrison, January, 1974

Station Street, Englishtown, January, 1974

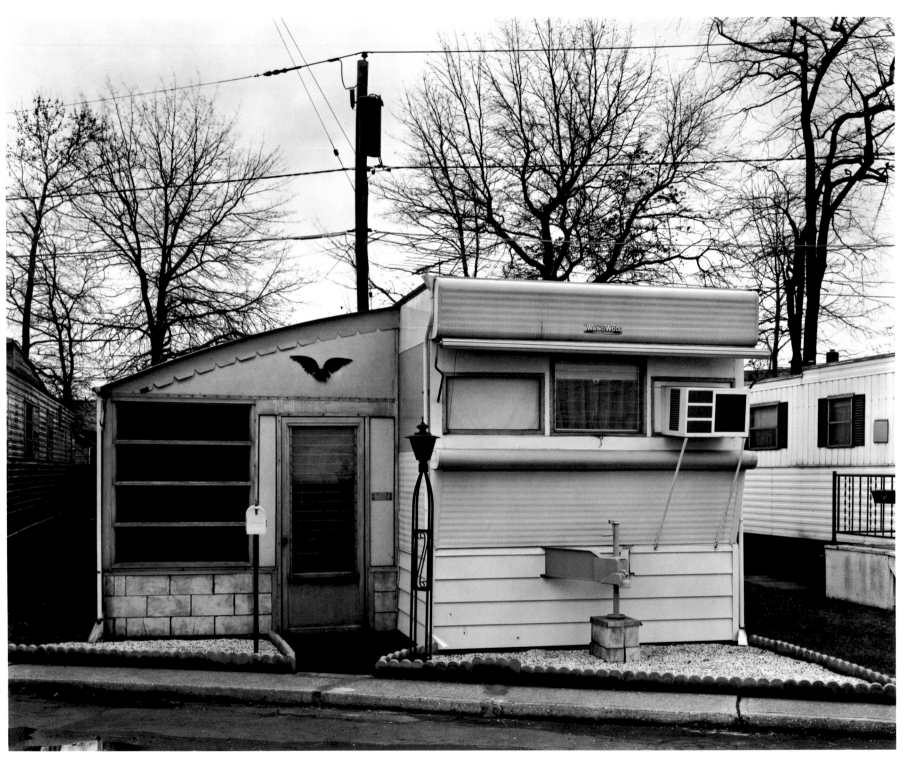

Mobile Home, Carteret Mobile Park, Carteret, November, 1973

Garris' General Store, Stillwater, August, 1973

William Stickel Memorial Bridge, Newark, March, 1974

Hudson Street, Phillipsburg, June, 1973

Wall, Chestnut Street, Newark, May, 1967

Billboard, Route #22, Hillside, July, 1974

The Beverage Shop, East Cherry Street, Rahway, May, 1973

Motel Sign, Route #130, Windsor, April, 1973

The Reformed Church, High Bridge, April, 1974

Holy Sepulchre Cemetery, Newark, April, 1974

Junked Cars, Naporano Wrecking Company, Newark, April, 1973

Telephone Booth, 3 A.M., St. Georges Avenue, Rahway, June, 1974